TORONTO

Welcome to Canada's largest, most dynamic, and most diverse city - Toronto! Located on the shores of Lake Ontario in southern Ontario, Toronto offers visitors all kinds of interesting and enjoyable opportunities to explore our history and culture as well as to shop, take in sports events, or just relax within a sophisticated and cosmopolitan environment. In the pages below, we will take you on a tour of this exciting metropolis where almost 3,000,000 people live. We will visit the city's historic and modern attractions, drop in on the places Torontonians go when they want to enjoy themselves or find inspiration, and generally have a good time.

But first, some history.

Toronto's origins go back thousands of years to the last ice age. As the great ice sheets slowly retreated northwards, small bands of hunter-gatherers migrated into southern Ontario. Back then - roughly 8000 BC - the environment was similar to Canada's modern arctic and sub-arctic climate. Over the next 5000 years, Ontario warmed to resemble the essentially modern temperatures of today, with cold winters and hot, often humid summers.

The indigenous peoples adapted to their changing environment, and eventually, about 900 AD, signifi-cant horticultural crops began to be grown in the region. Corn, beans, squash and other cultigens introduced from the southwest allowed the population to grow over subsequent centuries. A typical Ontario Iroquoian village in the early 17th century, when European explorers first reached Toronto, consisted of large, bark-covered longhouses, each of which was home for several families. Palisades often protected the village, beyond which lay the community's cultivated fields. Several hundred people usually lived in one village, and some housed as many as 2000.

The French maintained a trading post in Toronto in the 1720s and again in the 1750s in order to purchase some of the high quality furs the aboriginal people otherwise transported from the north to the British trading posts southeast of Lake Ontario. After the fall of Quebec in 1759 and the transfer of Canada to British rule in 1763, Toronto saw little European activity aside from the endeavours of a few fur traders and a some United Empire Loyalists who settled here as refugees from the American Revolution of 1775-83. In 1787 the British government bought the Toronto region for £1700 in cash and goods from the local natives. The urban settlement of Toronto began a few years later at Fort York in 1793.

Toronto from the southwest.

From 1793 to 1834, Toronto was called 'York,' or, as its detractors in the rival towns of Kingston and Niagara said, 'Muddy York' in contempt of its notoriously awful streets. York grew slowly as a small government and garrison town - only 750 people lived here in 1812. However, the great influx of immigrants from Britain after the end of the Napoleonic Wars in 1815 saw York's fortunes change as people fled the severe dislocations in Europe for a new life in Canada. The neighbouring countryside filled with settlers as forest gave way to farms and as York became an important commercial centre for the surrounding region. In 1834, the town was incorporated as the 'City of Toronto' with a population of 9000. Settlement continued and by mid-century, 31,000 people lived in the 'Queen City' as Victorian Torontonians liked to call their community.

The railways arrived in Toronto in the 1850s, heralding the beginning of a period of rapid industrialization and growth. By 1911, 377,000 people lived in a city which had taken the lead as English Canada's cultural centre. Three years later, Canadians rallied to Britain's aid at the outbreak of the Great War of 1914-18. Torontonians contributed a disproportionately large percentage of soldiers to the Canadian Expeditionary Force, and the city's factories worked as they never had before to supply the gargantuan appetite of the allied war effort. The Great Depression of 1929-39 hit the city hard, but industry once again flourished after 1939 as factories re-opened to meet the needs of a nation at war and as Canadian soldiers sailed to Europe for the second time in the 20th century.

Toronto emerged from World War II as a prosperous community of 696,000. It was also, to put it mildly, dull. One wit thought the city 'a good place in which to mind your own business.' However, all that was about to change. Tens of thousands of people from all over the world, first from continental Europe, then Asia, the Caribbean, and elsewhere, poured into the city and changed it dramatically. From a place where you could not get a drink or go to a movie on a Sunday, and where 73% of Torontonians in 1951 were British or the descendants of British immigrants, Toronto burst all its old bounds to become arguably the most multicultural city in the world, blessed with a fabulous variety of cultural, recreational, and entertainment options, an astonishing variety of cuisines, and a vibrancy that all its citizens can enjoy no matter what their origins.

At the same time, Canada entered an age of post-war prosperity unprecedented in its history. Toronto was a particularly fortunate beneficiary of this affluence. Gradually, Toronto replaced Montreal as Canada's largest urban centre as financial, industrial, and other economic endeavours concentrated in the city on the shore of Lake Ontario where its citizens today live, work, and play in one of North America's safest, cleanest, and most dynamic communities.

This page: on the Toronto waterfront.
Opposite: the icon of modern Toronto: the CN Tower.

Opposite: looking northeast towards SkyDome and the CN Tower from one of the city's many marinas.
This page: the west downtown waterfront from the harbour.

Next two pages: bird's-eye-view of the downtown from the southwest.

SKYDOME

Big. That is the over-reaching image of SkyDome, Toronto's famous stadium which sits squarely on 5.1 hectares of redeveloped railway land south of Front Street between Spadina and University avenues. Big. That also is the word for the great 3.2 hectare retractable roof which makes this 50,000+ seat stadium usable all year round. That roof, a marvel of Canadian engineering, weighing as much as 3732 automobiles, takes only 20 minutes to open or close. Big. With its roof closed, a 31-storey building could fit inside. SkyDome's playing field, according to its promoters, can hold 743 Indian elephants (or 516 African ones), or eight Boeing 747s, or, if you like, the entirety of the Toronto Eaton Centre, the Roman Coliseum, or London's St Paul's Cathedral - take your pick! Big. SkyDome's Astroturf playing field is fastened together with 12.8 kilometres of zippers!

So what do you do with all that big-ness? Well, you have the Toronto Blue Jays call SkyDome home, and then cheer them on to win the World Series Baseball Championships. Or, you watch the not-quite-so-famous Toronto Argonauts in their quest for the golden fleece of Canadian football, the Grey Cup. Alternatively, you find escape in the funky world of Monster Trucks or Wrestlemania. Or you enjoy one of a

plethora of other events, from auto and dog shows, to track and field meets, to huge religious festivals. If it's entertainment you want, then you go to a performance by Madonna, the Rolling Stones, Bruce Springsteen, Frank Sinatra, Eurythmics, Sting, or the Moscow Circus - all of whom have appeared at SkyDome. Perhaps the weirdest events you could have attended since SkyDome opened in 1989 were mass gatherings of people to watch the final episode of favourite televisions shows, such as 'Star Trek,' on SkyDome's JumboTron, a kind of 336-square-metre television screen.

To host so many events at the rate of 6,000,000 visitors each year, SkyDome has to be a stellar model of efficiency and adaptability. The retractable roof is perhaps its most flexible element - giving patrons shelter from the wintry blast while allowing summertime visitors to bask in the sun or enjoy the evening breeze off Lake Ontario. Within the stadium itself, seating can be re-configured in 20 minutes to meet the different needs of baseball and football games. A 13,950-square-metre SkyTent complex can be assembled within the stadium to provide the more intimate ambience and the first-rate acoustics needed for concerts and similar events.

This page, upper: SkyDome with its roof closed and open.
This page lower and next page: gargantuan sculptures of
enthusiastic sports fans by artist Michael Snow.

SkyDome is much more than a stadium. Naturally enough, food is a key ingredient in its success. It boasts the largest McDonald's restaurant in North America, 79 additional McDonald's outlets, a Hard Rock Café, and other food services. It has its own health club, souvenir shops, banking machines, and a variety of businesses designed to maximize Sky-Dome's profitability.

You can enjoy an hour-long walking tour of SkyDome which includes a behind-the-scenes visit to the media centre and dressing rooms, as well as a stroll down on the playing field. Getting to SkyDome is easy via SkyWalk, a climate-controlled covered walkway which links SkyDome to Union Station 500 metres to the east with its excellent connections to the subway, commuter trains, and the railway.

One unique feature of SkyDome is its SkyDome Hotel, the first hotel to be integrated fully into a domed sports and entertainment facility. Seventy of its 348 rooms overlook the playing field from which guests can enjoy the events below. However, guests who start to feel romantic during a game should close the curtains lest they distract the thousands of sports fans outside their hotel room window!

THE RAILWAY LANDS

Look at the roof of SkyDome in the picture to your left. Then, let your eye move to the right to the first major street which runs from the bottom of the picture, then west (or up) towards Fort York. That is Front Street. All the land to the left or south of Front is lakefill. That's right - it's all artificial, including the land SkyDome and the CN Tower sit on! Back in the 1840s, the shoreline of Lake Ontario lapped at the southern edge of Front Street.

What happened?

In the 1850s, during a tremendous economic boom, the railways arrived in Toronto. The problem was that the downtown already was built-up but the railways needed large amounts of land for tracks, stations, and yards. At the same time, the coming of the railways meant that the port facilities had to be upgraded substantially to handle the increased opportunities to be exploited exporting Canadian lumber and wheat which now passed through the city in far greater quantities than ever before. As well, Toronto's emerging industries sought new downtown property close to the railway and port facilities. The solution simply was to fill in part of Toronto Harbour and create new land! Beginning in the 1850s, Toronto dumped vast quantities of earth and other fill into its harbour, thus moving the shoreline hundreds of metres to the south to meet its growing needs as it evolved into a major industrial and commercial city in a rapidly expanding country. By the 1920s, most of the filling on the Toronto waterfront had been completed.

The glory days of the industrial, port, and railway lands along the waterfront began to come to an end in the post World War II era. Industries moved out of the downtown core to the suburbs; railway travel dropped dramatically as Canadians flocked to their cars; and the Port of Toronto's business steadily declined. Slowly, much of the great industrial infrastructure of downtown Toronto no longer was needed. As a result, the railway lands gradually became available for new development. The CN Tower was one of the first new projects, followed by SkyDome and other facilities. In future years, the railway's old John Street Roundhouse, located near the CN Tower, will become a railway heritage centre, and most of the tracks along the rail corridor will disappear, to be replaced by offices, housing, parks, and the other amenities of urban life.

This page: the CN Tower.
Opposite: looking west from the CN Tower: SkyDome, Railway Lands, Fort York, then off towards Humber Bay and the horizon.

*Looking south across Toronto Harbour to the Island Airport.
Opposite: the CN Tower's SkyPod.*

Looking north into the downtown.

THE CN TOWER

The world's tallest building, at 553.3 metres, is the CN Tower in downtown Toronto, open daily to serve the 1,600,000 people who visit it annually. Most come for the view from the SkyPod, two-thirds of the way up the tower, accessible via exterior elevators that travel upwards at the rate of 360 metres per minute. From the SkyPod, you can enjoy the view from either enclosed or outdoor observation decks. One of the most dramatic ways of seeing the world from the tower, if you're bold enough, is from the exterior, glass-floored observation deck, located 342 metres above ground! Naturally enough, the glass floor is strongly over-built. The CN Tower people say it will hold the weight of 14 hippopotamuses; although one suspects it might be difficult to convince the hippos to venture out on to it.

If you want to go even higher than the SkyPod, you can go to the Space Deck at 447 metres above ground, the world's tallest observation deck with a 160-kilometre view. Because of its altitude and position below the tower's communications antenna, you might feel some subtle movement while you are up there. Don't be alarmed. The CN Tower has been designed to be flexible, and therefore able to withstand the highest winds and other natural pressures Toronto is ever likely to face.

Down on the ground, the CN tower hosts a variety of high-tech amusements which it updates on a regular basis, such as virtual reality attractions, motion simulation theatres, laser tag, as well as a fast food court and other features. There also are a variety of facilities back up in the air to cater to your needs and interests. One is the famous environmental attraction, EcoDeck, with its award-winning interactive exhibits and theatres. Another is the recently-redecorated revolving restaurant. With its 300-label 'wine cellar in the sky,' the restaurant is open for lunch and dinner daily, brunch on Sundays, and weekday breakfasts during the summer. A short staircase away is Horizons Bar. By day, it serves light meals and refreshments, while at night, you can try your luck in the world's highest singles bar.

The CN Tower was built by Canadian National Railways between 1973 and 1976 as a communications tower. Today, a large number of television and radio stations, such as those operated by the Canadian Broadcasting Corporation, broadcast from the tower while other companies provide communications services to their clients from the tower using a variety of technologies.

The CN Tower is located between Front Street on the north, Lake Shore Boulevard on the south; Spadina Avenue on the west, and York Street on the east. The covered 500-metre SkyWalk between Union Stations and SkyDome provides protected pedestrian access to the tower.

Opposite: SkyDome and the CN Tower from the southwest.
This page: looking out from the CN Tower.

Next two pages: top: a rough day on Lake Ontario.
Bottom and opposite: the downtown business core.

Opposite: upper: the Power Plant Art Gallery;
lower: the quayside where you can board one of a number
of watercraft for a pleasant cruise around the harbour.

One of the many marinas and yacht clubs on the waterfront.

HARBOURFRONT AND QUEEN'S QUAY

Originally, the Harbourfront area was the centre of Toronto's industrial docklands. By the late 1960s, the region had become a wasteland of abandoned and under-utilized industrial buildings. Beginning in 1972, under the patronage of the federal government, this dead area was revitalized into a recreational and cultural attraction which now draws 3,000,000 visitors annually. Today, most people who visit Harbourfront (located along Queen's Quay between York Street and Spadina Avenue) come to enjoy a popular summertime destination, where they can enjoy the sun by the waterside, dock their boat after a day's sailing around the harbour and islands, do some shopping at Queen's Quay Terminal, listen to an outdoor concert, take a charter cruise, or send their kids to its famous children's cultural and recreational programmes. One popular destination is the Harbourfront Antique Market (at 390 Queen's Quay West), home of dozens of dealers who sell a plethora of goods, but with an emphasis on early 20th-century furniture and memorabilia.

Beyond these pleasures, Harbourfront also offers an enormous range of cultural opportunities. At the heart of these efforts are the Power Plant and the Du Maurier Theatre. The Power Plant at 231 Queen's Quay West is a non-collecting gallery devoted to the presentation of contemporary art, created by both local and international artists. The Du Maurier Theatre beside the Power Plant is a 420-seat flexible performance space dedicated to the presentation of music and new theatre. Not far away, are Molson Place, an outdoor concert facility with a dramatic glass roof, and the York Quay Centre with an assortment of cultural facilities. Harbourfront also is well-known for its international theatre, film, dance, and literary festivals as well as its ethnocultural celebrations and its adult craft and art classes.

Opposite: the Harbourfront experience: waterside recreation, cultural events, and shopping at Queen's Quay Terminal.

A vintage ferry whisks you across the harbour to the bucolic world of the Toronto Islands.

TORONTO ISLANDS

The Toronto Islands on the south side of Toronto Harbour give the city a unique, waterfront retreat from the summer's heat. They were formed thousands of years ago as sand and earth from the Scarborough Bluffs east of Toronto fell into Lake Ontario, to be washed west where they accumulated to form the islands. Originally the islands were a peninsula attached to the mainland at their east end, but erosion and storms opened up a gap - the Eastern Gap - in the 1850s, thus permanently separating them from the mainland.

Today, the islands are a good place to bring your family in search of a quieter, lakeside experience. Once you get there, you can rent a bicycle (or bring your own) and cycle the islands along an extensive system of paved trails. If you walk, and get tired, there is a trackless train to take you around the sights between April and October. Or, you can rent a canoe or a paddleboat and explore the large number of channels and lagoons, or walk over to the south side to enjoy one of the beaches by the lake. On Centre Island, you can cross over the historic Manitou Bridge and walk south along the flower-lined Av-

enue of the Islands which ends in a 160-metre pier overlooking Lake Ontario.

There also are some historical attractions to see. The most famous is the Gibraltar Point Lighthouse, close to Hanlan's Point. Built in 1808, the stone building is one of the city's oldest structures and is said to be haunted by the ghost of its first lighthouse keeper, murdered in 1815 by some soldiers from Fort York. Over at the east end of the islands is a little village on Ward's Island where several hundred people live in a green cottage paradise within a 15-minute ferry commute of the downtown. Nearby is an 1884 church, St-Andrew's-by-the-Lake. These buildings are about all that remain of what was once a thriving waterside community of several thousand, complete with hotels and other attractions which flourished in the late 19th and early 20th centuries. There even was a baseball stadium at Hanlan's Point where Babe Ruth played in the 1920s. Most of those structures that survived the years were torn down in the 1950s and 1960s in order to create the parklands that grace the islands today.

This page and opposite: in and around Toronto Harbour, sheltered from Lake Ontario by the Toronto Islands.

The Ferries

Torontonians have sought relaxation on the islands by taking a ferry across Toronto Harbour since the 19th century. Today, the tradition lives on with frequent service from the Ferry Docks on Queen's Quay near the foot of Bay Street. The short trip is an excellent way to enjoy the harbour sights. Ward's Island, at the eastern end of the islands, boasts a charming lakeside community where residents live all year by the peaceful shore of Lake Ontario. Centre Island, with its varied amusements, is the most popular destination for people looking for fun, while Hanlan's Point, to the west, is the destination of those who want a quieter waterside retreat.

27

Centreville

Centreville on Centre Island is a privately-run amusement park offering rides, restaurants, shops, and games within a c.1900 theme setting. There is a merry-go-round, ferris wheel, miniature train, barrel ride, and bumper cars, all of which were developed primarily for children as were Centreville's snack bars and ice cream parlour. Close by is Far Enough Farm, the publicly-operated home of a friendly assortment of barnyard animals who you can visit and pet for free.

Also on the island are various playgrounds and wading pools for you and your children to enjoy as well as two licensed restaurants. One is the Paradise at the Centre Island Ferry Dock with its outdoor patio and panoramic view of downtown Toronto. The other is the Iroquois, located near Centreville and the Manitou Bridge. As well, the islands have extensive mooring facilities for pleasure boats and a number of yacht clubs.

Opposite: upper: the Avenue of the Islands; bottom: canoeing on the Regatta Course.
This page: the simple pleasures of Centreville.

Next two pages: the city as seen from one of the ferries.

TORONTO HARBOUR

It was Toronto's defensible and sheltered harbour that led the British to establish an urban community at Toronto in 1793. Back then, the Toronto Islands were a long peninsula joined to the mainland at their east end. Thus, the harbour was a kind of bay, with the mainland and peninsula providing a large, sheltered anchorage. (The eastern gap opened up in the middle of the 19th century.)

As the 19th century progressed, the harbour grew as a port and industrial facility, particularly after the coming of the railways in the 1850s. When the St Lawrence Seaway opened in 1959, Torontonians expected that growth to continue because large ocean-going ships could now reach the Great Lakes. However, the expansion never came, and the last few decades have seen the port and industrial facilities decline steadily as Toronto has moved into a post-industrial economic world. Today, the industrial port facilities of Toronto Harbour are concentrated at the east end of the harbour at the foot of Cherry Street. The rest of the harbour lands have been, or are being, developed for recreational, residential, and commercial use, with Harbourfront being the most famous project.

The striking contrast of a peaceful body of water in front of a dynamic city.

33

ONTARIO PLACE

Located in Lake Ontario, just south of Exhibition Place and a little west of the downtown, is Ontario Place, a waterside amusement park operated by the Government of Ontario. Opened in 1971 on three artificial islands, this 38-hectare park has become one of the city's recreational institutions, offering a multiplicity of services to the public every summer (with some limited off-season programming as well). One of the best attractions at Ontario Place is the Cinesphere, an enormous triodetic-domed IMAX theatre where you can watch dramatic movies on one of the world's largest movie screens. It's a fabulous experience, not to be missed. Another great attraction, aimed at the historically-minded, is HMCS *Haida*, Canada's most famous World War II warship, now open as a floating naval museum. More recently, Ontario Place opened the Molson Amphitheatre, a outdoor concert venue presenting different musical productions. You can reserve a place in advance in one of the Amphitheatre's 9000 fixed seats, or you can enjoy the presentation from one of the 7000 casual spaces available on the nearby lawns. As well, a marina, golf courses, canoe rentals, water slides, a wilderness adventure ride, pedal boats, bumper boats, children's village, bungy jumping, restaurants, bars, laser shows, annual festivals, and all sorts of other amusements flesh out Ontario Place's appeal to guarantee a fun-filled and care-free day for the whole family.

This page and opposite: the pleasures of Ontario Place.

EXHIBITION PLACE

Exhibition Place, located between Strachan Avenue on the east and Dufferin Street on the west, north of Lake Shore Boulevard, is one of Toronto's most venerable institutions. Dating back more than a century, the flagship event of the year is the Canadian National Exhibition held late every summer. The CNE, or 'the Ex' as Torontonians call it, takes up the entire grounds, offering visitors a midway, exhibits, crafts, concerts, and all the enticements of a carnival atmosphere which harkens back to the CNE's roots as an overgrown country fair.

Another classic event at Exhibition Place is the annual Royal Winter Fair, held late in the autumn, where Torontonians can sample Ontario's rural roots through the fair's horse shows and other presentations. In July, Exhibition Place hosts the Molson Indy for racing car enthusiasts, and throughout the year trade shows and other events draw people to the site. As well, Exhibition Place is home to a monument commemorating the French fur trade post which stood on the grounds in the 1750s, Scadding Cabin (a small log home from the 1790s), and the Marine Museum of Upper Canada, housed in an 1841 British army building.

This page: early 20th-century fair buildings.
Opposite, upper: the Princes' Gates at the east entrance; lower: inside the CNE grounds.

The highlight of Exhibition Place's year is the Canadian National Exhibition, which runs from mid-August to early September. Exhibits, art, horse shows, shopping, and the joys of a midway carnival mark this favourite Toronto event.

HISTORIC FORT YORK

Fort York, located a few blocks west of SkyDome, is the city's oldest and most important historic site. The founding of modern urban Toronto took place at the fort in 1793 when the British built a garrison during a period of threatened American invasion. Because of the crisis, they decided to establish a naval base in Toronto's defensible harbour to control Lake Ontario. Civilian settlement followed, and a new community, 'York,' began to grow. Back then, Fort York was ideally sited to protect the entrance to Toronto Harbour because it sat on the shore of Lake Ontario. Today, the fort sits 900 metres inland. But it is not the fort that has moved - it's the lake! All the land south of Fort York is fill placed there between the 1850s and the 1920s.

In 1812, the United States declared war on Great Britain and invaded Canada. York was attacked three times during the War of 1812. The first, and bloodiest attack, occurred on 27 April 1813 when the United States Navy carried an invading army across Lake Ontario to assault the colonial capital. After a six-hour battle, the badly outnumbered British, Canadian, Mississauga, and Ojibway defenders were forced to abandon the town to the Americans.

Among the battle's casualties was the famous American explorer, Brigadier-General Zebulon Pike, who fell mortally-wounded at the moment of victory. The Americans occupied York for a week, destroyed its defences, looted homes, and burned both the governor's home at the fort and the parliament buildings in the town. A year later, the British retaliated when they captured Washington and burned the White House and Congress.

The Americans returned a second time in July 1813 to burn the undefended barracks at Fort York. Shortly afterwards, the British re-occupied Toronto and rebuilt the fort - today's Fort York. It was attacked in August 1814, but its guns chased away the American ships and saved the town from a third occupation.

After defending Canada successfully in the War of 1812, the British army continued to garrison Fort York until 1870. There were numerous periods of tension during this time. The fort was re-armed and strengthened during two of them: the Rebellion of 1837 when an attempt was made to overthrow the government; and in the 1860s when Anglo-American relations seemed to be degenerating towards hostilities as a consequence of the American Civil War.

Fort York in 1860.

Opposite: looking east past an original 1813 Blockhouse towards the modern skyline.

In 1870, the British army left Toronto and transferred responsibility for defence to the new Dominion of Canada, created in 1867. Canadian soldiers maintained the harbour defences until the 1880s. However, Fort York's military life did not end at that point. It continued to serve the needs of the Toronto garrison for barracks, storage, and training until the 1930s. Then, in 1934, after a two-year restoration, the fort reopened as a historic site museum operated by the City of Toronto.

Today, Fort York's defensive walls surround Canada's largest collection of original War of 1812 buildings. Exhibits inside these structures for your enjoyment include restored areas such as barracks, kitchens, and magazines, plus a number of museum displays which explore Canada's turbulent military past.

Upper: the 1815 Officers Brick Barracks and Mess; lower: a British howitzer sent to Canada during the Anglo-American crisis of the 1860s.

Next page: upper: an interior view of an 1815 Soldiers Barracks; lower: a museum display of a Canadian militiaman of 1793 and a British soldier of 1812.

The garrison stationed at the fort included many famous British and Canadian regiments, along with the soldiers' wives and children. A single barrack room might house 25 soldiers in 1815, plus five or six women and their children! There was a school at the fort as well as a 'lying-in' room for soldiers' wives to use at childbirth. Later in the 19th century, barracks improved, first by reducing the number of people crammed into each room, then by separating married from single soldiers. In contrast, the officers quarters was a far more comfortable place, as befitted the middle and upper level origins of most army officers.

Fort York is located just west of the downtown core, on Garrison Road, off Fleet Street, between Bathurst Street and Strachan Avenue. The Bathurst 511 Streetcar passes close to the fort. Unlike most attractions in Toronto, parking at Fort York is free!

Opposite: the Officers Quarters are restored to look the way they did in the 1830s: top: the dining room; below: a captain's bedroom.
This page: top: at work in the mess kitchen; below: the mess sergeant's room.

This page: the heart of Chinatown radiates north and south from Dundas Street on Spadina Avenue, and east of Spadina on Dundas. Opposite: Chinatown and Kensington Market are the places to shop for some of the freshest and most interesting foods in the city.

KENSINGTON MARKET AND CHINATOWN

Kensington Market and Chinatown are associated with the city's growing multicultural heritage as it was in this part of Toronto that many immigrant groups first settled when they came to Canada. Today, for example, Chinese businesses and restaurants occupy an area that a century ago was home for recently-arrived Jewish and other eastern European immigrants. Meanwhile, more recent newcomers are mixing a Vietnamese character into Chinatown's personality so that you can savour the best cuisine of both China and Vietnam within one compact area.

Kensington Market likewise presents the story of successive waves of immigrants over the last century through the presence of businesses of European, Caribbean, and Latin American origin. Kensington Market is not a traditional single-site market. Rather, it consists of a number of side streets just west of Spadina Avenue, between Dundas and College streets, that originally were built for residential use but which are now dominated by small shops. The result is a bustling and crowded environment where you can sample the cultures of the world, find great bargains, and enjoy terrific food in a part of the city Torontonians know well but where tourists are noticeably absent.

GEORGE BROWN HOUSE AND QUEEN STREET WEST

George Brown House is a good example of a prominent Toronto home of the 1870s. Today, you may drop in and admire the principal ground floor rooms. George Brown was a noted politician and editor of the *Globe*, now the *Globe and Mail*, Canada's most prestigious newspaper. Brown is best remembered for his role in helping to bring about the Canadian Confederation of 1867 which saw three British colonies - Nova Scotia, New Brunswick, and Canada (now Ontario and Quebec) - unite to form a country within the British Empire - the Dominion of Canada. Over subsequent years, more of the British possessions in North America joined Canada to form what is now the second largest country in the world after Russia.

Queen Street West, with its line of 19th-century facades, lies a few blocks south of George Brown House. This stretch of Queen, west of University Avenue, is the home of fashion designers, poets, musicians, and a concentration of Toronto's young and rebellious set. The restaurants, clubs, and shops along Queen cater to a wide variety of alternative or specialized tastes.

Top: George Brown House at 50 Baldwin Street, north of Dundas Street; bottom: the Black Bull Tavern on Queen Street West.

Henry Moore's 'Two Large Forms' stands proudly outside the Art Gallery of Ontario at 317 Dundas Street West, between University and Spadina avenues.

ART GALLERY OF ONTARIO

One of Canada's great fine art museums is the Art Gallery of Ontario - a Toronto resource that you should not miss! Recently renovated, the AGO offers visitors an exceptional opportunity to enjoy great art or partake in the gallery's many programmes, ranging from lectures, to jazz performances, to film festivals.

Some of the gallery's many highlights include its 17th-century Dutch masters, 19th-century Impressionists, its Henry Moore collection of 143 sculptures and 700 works on paper, and its Canadian collection, including a wonderful compendium of paintings by the famous 'Group of Seven' who dominated art in this country during the first half of the 20th century. Beyond these highlights, the AGO presents Inuit sculptures, 20th-century American art, a wide-ranging prints and drawings collection, and a truly exciting series of temporary and travelling exhibits.

In addition, the AGO incorporates a charming Georgian house - the Grange - built c.1817 and now run as a living history museum. The AGO also boasts a good restaurant, a family-oriented activity centre, and a huge gift shop.

This page and opposite: Roy Thompson Hall, on King Street, west of University Avenue, stands across the street from St Andrew's Presbyterian Church of 1874-5.

ROY THOMPSON HALL

Excellent music has been a Toronto hallmark for generations. Today, with the Toronto Symphony, Tafelmusic, the Toronto Mendelssohn Choir and a variety of other renowned orchestras, choirs, and soloists calling Toronto home, and with the city located squarely on the international touring circuit, you never need to spend a quiet evening in Toronto if you would rather go to a great concert instead. Of the various concert venues in the city, the most famous is Roy Thompson Hall.

Since opening in 1982, Thompson Hall, with its brilliant acoustic engineering, great pipe organ, and handsome modern interior, has been the home of the Toronto Symphony as well as the concert hall of choice of the international artists who visit the city. Just south of Thompson Hall is the CBC Broadcast Centre with its new Glenn Gould Studio which also boasts an active programme of excellent performances. The people who manage Thompson Hall also operate Massey Hall, an 1894 concert hall located a few blocks away on Shuter Street at Yonge near the Eaton Centre, a building noted for its excellent acoustics and its 'Moorish' interior design which formerly was the Toronto Symphony's home and which now plays host to different performers on a very busy schedule.

NEW CITY HALL

New City Hall, at 100 Queen Street West, is a jewel in the crown of modernist architecture. Designed by the Finnish architect Viljo Revell, New City Hall opened in 1965. Here Toronto City Council meets in the thing that looks like a flying saucer in the middle of the building. (Perhaps politicians really do come from Mars.) Back in 1956, Mayor Nathan Phillips convinced Toronto City Council to hold an international competition to select a design for its new civic headquarters. By the time the competition ended, Toronto had received 520 submissions from 42 countries. In 1958, Viljo Revell from Helsinki was proclaimed the winner by the jury of five internationally known architects. Construction began in 1961 on the design which features two curved office towers and the domed council chamber. Revell intended the council chamber to represent the democratically-elected 'eye' at the centre of the city bureaucracy.

Nathan Phillips Square in front of City Hall has become an important civic space over the years, hosting annual events such as a summer art festival and numerous concerts, in addition to civic celebrations and protests. Various monuments and architectural features surround city hall. One of them is Henry Moore's free-form bronze statue, 'Three-Way Piece Number Two' (a.k.a. 'The Archer') which Viljo Revell chose specifically for the front of city hall. Another is the 1984 Peace Garden, with its Japanese-inspired motifs and eternal flame.

On the west side of this modernist masterpiece is a much older architectural treasure, Osgoode Hall, with its famous library and law courts. Don't miss this splendid building, parts of which go back to 1829, and don't be afraid to wander inside and enjoy its decorative delights, or even sit in one of the public galleries of the law courts. One of the more amusing features of Osgoode Hall is the 1866 fence which surrounds the building, complete with specially-designed gates to keep cows out! (Back then this was a quiet suburban area.) A little farther west on Queen Street, across University Avenue, is a restored historic site, Campbell House from the 1820s which you can visit.

This page and opposite: New City Hall and Nathan Phillips Square, on Queen Street, between Bay Street and University Avenue.

OLD CITY HALL

Just east of New City Hall, at Queen and Bay, is Toronto's third city hall, a remarkable Romanesque Revival building which opened in 1899 and which now is known as Old City Hall. Its exterior comprises a handsome combination of grey Credit River Valley stone (located in southern Ontario) and carved brownstone from New Brunswick. If you look up near the roof-line, you can see a number of grimacing faces carved into the stone which are said to have been the architect's effort to lampoon the city's politicians who made his life miserable during construction of the building. Inside the light grey and white marble interior, visitors can savour various architectural features, including a large stained glass window created in tribute to late Victorian notions of progress and civic pride. Today, Old City Hall is used mainly for low-level courts. Thus, you might find yourself passing the incongruous sight of happy couples on their way to civic weddings and glum petty criminals proceeding to meet their fate at the hands of the provincial court judges.

This page: the reflecting pool in front of New City Hall: a place to cool your heels during summer's heat; in winter, a place to go ice skating.
Opposite: Old City Hall, located between the Eaton Centre and New City Hall.

This page: Toronto's brashest street - Yonge, as seen near Dundas Street.
Opposite: Toronto's great downtown mall, the Eaton Centre on Yonge, between Dundas and Queen streets.

YONGE STREET AND THE EATON CENTRE

Yonge Street was created back in the 1790s as a military road which cut through the primaeval forest to connect Toronto to the north. Today, this intensely urban and impertinent street bears virtually no resemblance to its historic origins. Instead, particularly south of Bloor Street, this is where you go to see younger Torontonians enjoying themselves in the evening, visit a bar to hear one of the innumerable bands in the city, eat junk food, shop, go to the movies, or pursue the needs of the libido. (Watch your wallet!)

North of Bloor, Yonge Street changes, becoming decidedly more affluent with quite good shops and restaurants, particularly near the intersections of Yonge and St Clair Avenue, and Yonge and Eglinton Avenue. Back downtown, at Yonge and Dundas streets, you can enjoy the city's premier attraction for both tourists and residents: a mall, the Eaton Centre with its 320 shops in the heart of the city. The Province of Ontario has a tourist office in the centre where you can obtain literature and information on attractions throughout Ontario.

THE THEATRES

Toronto is a great city for theatre, whether you prefer small, *avant-garde* productions, famous corps such as the National Ballet of Canada and the Canadian Opera Company, or large international musicals by Andrew Lloyd Weber and his contemporaries. To find out about what's on in Toronto, consult the local newspapers or the free entertainment tabloids which can be picked up at many of the city's restaurants, libraries, or other public places.

Some of the major theatres, such as the O'Keefe/Hummingbird Centre or the Princess of Wales Theatre at 300 King Street West, are modern facilities while others, such as Pantages, the Royal Alexandra, and the Elgin and Winter Garden Theatres on Yonge near Queen, were built in the early 20th century and have been restored to their former glory in recent years. Smaller theatres and performing halls run the gamut from dingy little church basements to quite good facilities, such as the Hart House Theatre and the concert facilities in the Edward Johnson Building, both at the University of Toronto.

Opposite: brassy Yonge Street at Dundas.
This page (clockwise): three theatres: Pantages on Yonge near Dundas Street; the O'Keefe/Hummingbird Centre at Yonge and Front streets; and the Royal Alexandra on King Street, west of University Avenue.

HOCKEY HALL OF FAME, UNION STATION, AND THE FINANCIAL DISTRICT

One of Toronto's newest attractions is the Hockey Hall of Fame, a high-tech museum dedicated to Canada's favourite sport, and located in a historic bank at Yonge and Front streets. (Toronto's great shrine to hockey, the 1931 Maple Leaf Gardens, is only a few subway stops away, just east of the corner of Yonge and College streets.)

Just west of the Hockey Hall of Fame, at Bay and Front streets, is Union Station, Toronto's main railway terminal. The building itself is a Classical Revival structure, and its great hall - worth a look - is the largest room in Canada. North of Union Station lies the heart of the city's financial district, marked by its skyscrapers, all of which are connected to each other through a system of underground shopping malls. Architecturally, the most interesting office buildings are the 1973-7 Royal Bank Plaza with its gold - yes real gold - covered windows at Bay and Front, the soaring interior galleria of the 1993 BCE Place at 181 Bay Street, Mies van der Rohe's international style 1964-71 Toronto Dominion Centre at 55 King Street West, and the 1929-31 Bank of Commerce at 25 King Street West.

This page: in and about Union Station and its neighbourhood.

Opposite: top: the Hockey Hall of Fame, located in the 1885-6 Beaux Arts Bank of Montreal; bottom: a statue honouring immigrants to Toronto in front of the 1927 Union Station across the street from the 1928-9 Royal York Hotel.

The 1891-2 Flat Iron Building at Wellington and Front streets; the interior of St James Cathedral at King and Church streets; and St James Park beside the cathedral.

ST JAMES CATHEDRAL

St James Anglican Cathedral is one of several magnificent churches in Toronto, along with St Michael's Roman Catholic Cathedral and Metropolitan United Church, both located a short distance north of St James. St James has its origins in the 1790s when the government set aside the land on which it sits for the Church of England. A small frame church opened in 1807, which itself was replaced with a large masonry building in 1833. Fires destroyed that building and its successor, which allowed the congregation to build the present building in the English Gothic Revival style so popular among mid-19th-century Victorians. Today's cathedral, which opened in 1853, boasts Canada's tallest steeple, beautiful stained glass windows created in Toronto, New York, Britain, and Germany, a glorious organ, and various memorials to Toronto's old Anglican elite. Worship occurs daily; and on Sundays, you can attend the earlier service using the modern liturgy, or the traditional Book of Common Prayer service - complete with a cathedral men and boys choir - at 11:00 a.m.

In and about St Lawrence Market at Front and Jarvis streets.

ST LAWRENCE MARKET

A short distance from St James Cathedral is St Lawrence Market. A farmers' market has been held here continuously since 1802. Today, there are two market buildings: the historic south market, open Tuesdays to Saturdays with permanent stalls on two floors, and the modern north farmers' market open on Saturdays. With its street buskers, great food, and wonderful atmosphere, this is the place to come on Saturday mornings to shop, have breakfast, and mingle with the natives. Inside the south market is Toronto's 1844-5 City Hall, now the home of the city-run Market Gallery which presents changing historical exhibits throughout the year.

The whole district around the market, particularly between Jarvis and Yonge streets, is historic, with various old buildings and interesting shops. Some of the highlights include St Lawrence Hall at 157 King Street, built in 1850; St James Park beside the cathedral, with its odd combination of street people and a pretty little Victorian flower garden; a little sculpture garden across the street from the cathedral; and the Victorian architecture on both Toronto Street (north of King, between Yonge and Church) and along Front Street between St Lawrence Market and Yonge.

The conservatory and palm house of Allan Gardens, a few blocks east of Yonge Street at Carlton Avenue and Jarvis Street.

ALLAN GARDENS CONSERVATORY

Allan Gardens dates back to 1858 when George Allan, a local politician and cultural leader, offered some land for development as a public garden. Two years later, the Prince of Wales (later King Edward VII) opened the gardens during his visit to Toronto. From then, the City of Toronto and various horticultural groups developed the park for the enjoyment of all those who love flowers (particularly for those desirous of a temporary respite from the dull greyness of a Toronto winter).

In the 1890s, the city replaced the older conservatory facilities with the present structure, built in the British glass and metal greenhouse tradition, which the city then enlarged over the years. Today, the gardens sit as an oasis of Victorian tranquillity in an otherwise depressed neighbourhood. A visit to the conservatory today transports visitors through several distinct ecological zones, from the dry beauty of the world of cacti, through the glorious plants of temperate climes, and on to the lush realms inhabited by tropical vegetation.

The Ontario Legislative Building at Queen's Park, just north of College Street, at the head of University Avenue, near the University of Toronto.

ONTARIO PARLIAMENT BUILDINGS

Canada is a parliamentary democracy with a federal system of government, consisting of a central government in Ottawa as well as provincial and territorial governments. As the capital of Ontario, Toronto is home for the provincial legislative assembly where three parties dominate Ontario's political landscape: the New Democrats on the left, the Liberals at the centre, and the Progressive Conservatives on the right.

The home of the Ontario government since 1893 has been the grand Richardsonian Romanesque Parliament Buildings in Queen's Park. Normally open to the public, you may stroll through the buildings and grounds, view the exhibits on the history of parliament, or take a guided tour. When the legislature is in session, you can get a pass at the main information desk to watch the proceedings from the public galleries. The best time to go is 'Question Period' when the opposition parties do their best to embarrass the government party with questions designed to expose the government's stupidity for that evening's television news and the next morning's papers!

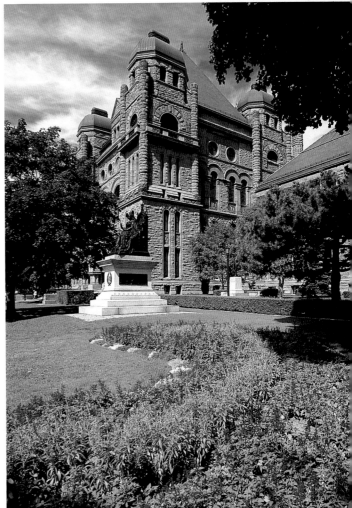

The Romanesque architecture of the 1856-9 University College.
Opposite: 20th-century Collegiate Gothic at Trinity College.

THE UNIVERSITY OF TORONTO

Founded in 1827, the University of Toronto is Canada's largest and most famous university, home of 53,000 students, 11,000 faculty and staff, and some of Canada's most prominent scientists and scholars. Today, through 30 departments, the university offers more than 300 programmes and an enormous range of courses - 2,000 in the Faculty of Arts and Sciences alone - to its undergraduate, graduate, and part-time students.

Don't hesitate to walk into the buildings at the U. of T. campus to have a look around. Some of the more interesting interiors are: the main room of the University of Toronto Book Store, the chapel and the dining hall at Trinity College, the second floor great rooms of University College, the chapel and library at Knox College, Hart House (and its art gallery), and the Sydney Fisher Rare Book Library (adjacent to the large Robarts Library) with its little exhibit gallery overlooking the rare book stacks in what is one of the city's finest modern interiors. In the summer, the university offers daily tours of the campus from Hart House. The University of Toronto takes up a large portion of the downtown area between Bloor Street on the north, College Street on the south, Spadina Avenue on the west and Bay Street on the east.

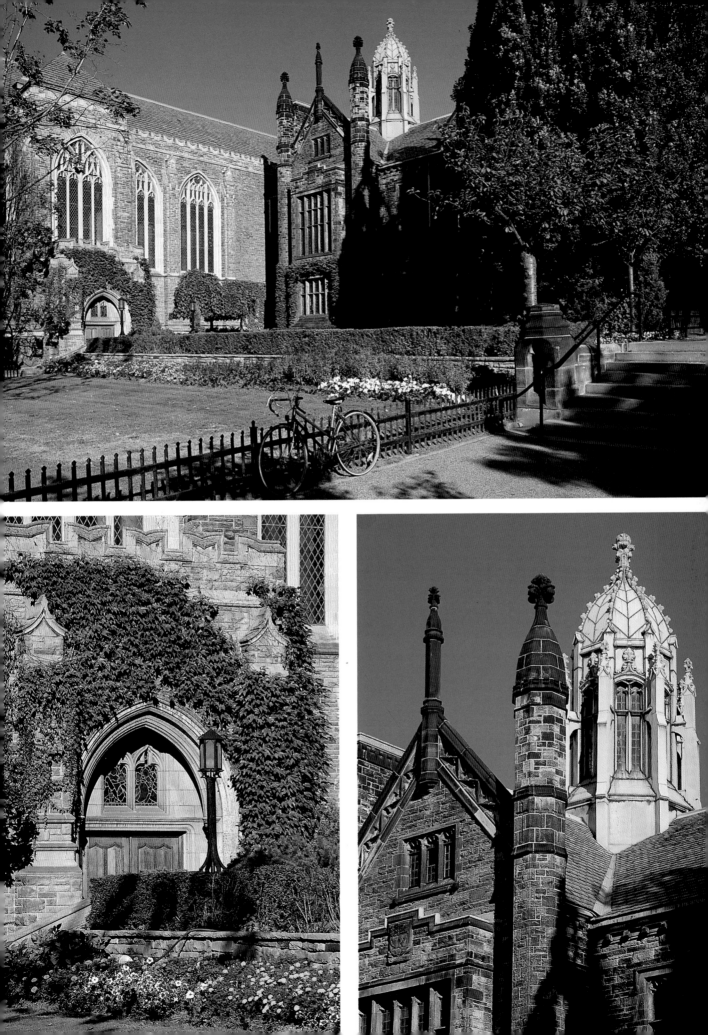

The Royal Ontario Museum on Queen's Park at Bloor Street.　　　　*Opposite: part of the ROM's magnificent Chinese collection.*

ROYAL ONTARIO MUSEUM

Canada's most prestigious museum is the Royal Ontario Museum. No visit to Toronto would be complete without a stop at the 'ROM,' one of the world's few multi-disciplinary museums which combines a rich collection of galleries devoted to art, archaeology, and science. Beyond galleries - spread over four floors and which easily will consume a day's viewing - the ROM has a children's discovery gallery, good gift shops, a cafeteria, and an excellent restaurant presided over by one of the city's most famous chefs. Canadian heritage is the focus of much of the basement area of the ROM. Galleries there explore aboriginal history, the European presence in Canada, contemporary culture, as well as other topics in temporary exhibits. One of the highlights in this part of the museum is Benjamin West's famous painting, *The Death of Wolfe*. One of the ground floor's central galleries is the 'Mankind Discovering' exhibit which examines how museums go about their scholarly endeavours. One of the more popular displays in 'Mankind Discovering,' especially among children, is an Egyptian mummy which ROM staff autopsied to discover fascinating details about the mummy's life, health, and death. The real treasures of the ground floor are to be found in the Chinese galleries, housing one of the western world's very best collections of Chinese artifacts. Also on the ground floor, but a bit out of the way, is a marvellous collection of gems and precious metals.

The second floor is devoted to the sciences. Naturally, the most popular galleries for children are those devoted to dinosaurs. But equally appealing are the 'bat cave' and the various exhibits devoted to Canadian and foreign animals, birds, amphibians, reptiles, and insects. The third floor galleries cover a wide range of cultures. The European galleries, focused largely on decorative arts from mediaeval times, include some splendid recreated period-room settings as well as collections of arms and armour, ceramics, and textiles. Other galleries on the third floor explore such themes as ancient Mesopotamia, Egypt, Nubia, and Iran; the Celtic world; Islamic civilizations; the Greeks, Etruscans, and Romans; and Byzantium.

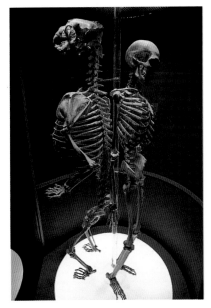

Some of the Royal Ontario Museum's many galleries.
This page: Dinosaurs and Evolution - the most popular galleries in the museum, presenting some of the world's finest specimens, with an emphasis on dinosaurs excavated in Canada.

Opposite: Chinese, Egyptian, Greek, and Roman galleries where you can trace the main currents of world civilizations.

Opposite: part of the Royal Ontario Museum's popular dinosaur galleries. This page: upper: The Bata Shoe Museum; lower: The George R. Gardiner Museum of Ceramic Art.

THE BATA SHOE MUSEUM AND THE GEORGE R. GARDINER MUSEUM OF CERAMIC ART

Toronto has a number of small museums and galleries, such as the Marine Museum of Upper Canada, the Market Gallery, and the Metropolitan Toronto Police Museum on College Street between Bay and Yonge streets. Two of the most famous specialized institutions are the Bata Shoe Museum and the George R. Gardiner Museum of Ceramic Art.

The Gardiner Museum is located across the street from the Royal Ontario Museum, and admission to the ROM includes access to the Gardiner. This treasure house of ceramic art features Italian majolica, English delftware, porcelains from England and the continent, and other examples of ceramic art, all within a series of very fine galleries. The Bata Shoe Museum sits two blocks west of the ROM, at Bloor and St George streets. With its 10,000 shoes, costumes, and other artifacts, supplemented by interactive exhibits and special programmes, the Bata Shoe Museum offers a unique opportunity to explore the world of shoes, which we take for granted, but which, upon study, provides enchanting opportunities to understand our own and foreign cultures through time.

From top to bottom: the 1879 Anglican Church of the Redeemer at the corner of Bloor Street and Avenue Road; Yorkville; and Edwardian architecture at the Yorkville Public Library of 1906-7 with the Victorian 1876 Yorkville Firehall in the background.

BLOOR STREET WEST AND YORKVILLE

The city's most upscale shopping district lies along Bloor Street West and in Yorkville. Bloor Street, running west from Yonge Street, is home to such prestigious stores as Holts where you can purchase the most fashionable consumer goods available in Canada. Yorkville consists of a number of streets north of Bloor, largely between Bay Street and Avenue Road, where old Victorian and Edwardian buildings have been converted into small specialty shops along with interesting restaurants and outdoor cafés. One of the often-overlooked aspects of Yorkville is its architecture, particularly north on Hazelton Avenue where you can spend half an hour enjoying an attractive collection of Victorian houses and public buildings.

Within Yorkville, at 55 Avenue Road, just north of Bloor Street, and located behind the street facades of Yorkville and Hazelton avenues, is Hazelton Lanes, a gem of a little mall where you can shop for a marvellous array of goods, fashions, and specialty items from some of the city's most exclusive shops or from the Toronto branches of such international companies as Ralph Lauren, Teuscher of Switzerland, and Turnbull and Asser. There also is one of the city's more interesting Vintages liquor stores in Hazelton Lanes and a very good classical CD shop.

LITTLE ITALY

Since 1945, tens of thousands of people from all over the world have poured into Toronto, making it one of the most multi-cultural cities in the world. Italians were the largest group of such immigrants, and today are the second most populous group after those of British origin in the city. As a result, the city has several 'Little Italies' where you can enjoy the joys of being Italian, from great restaurants, to soccer games, to cultural events. One of these little Italies lies along St Clair Avenue, east and west of Dufferin Street. Another (with a additional Portuguese accent) runs along College Street, west of Bathurst Street. Beyond these districts, Italian culture permeates much of the city, particularly in terms of shopping opportunities and fine restaurants located throughout Toronto.

As well as the Italians, other cultural groups have found a concentrated home along certain main streets in Toronto. The most famous of course is Chinatown near Dundas Street and Spadina Avenue. Others include the city's Greek neighbourhood, noted for its restaurants, on Danforth Avenue in and around Pape Avenue; a concentration of Polish restaurants and shops on Roncesvalles Avenue; a small but dynamic East Indian community on Gerrard at Coxwell; and the Jewish community focused in and around the suburban regions centred on Bathurst Street and Lawrence Avenue. Other ethnic groups also have a regional presence around Toronto, although they often are less obviously visible to the eye. For example, there is a concentration of Hungarian restaurants and specialty shops along Bloor Street between Spadina Avenue and Markham Street, but these are heavily intermixed with a large number of other restaurants and stores, both ethnic and Canadian. Other groups are represented more thinly on the urban landscape, but can be found. Toronto has, for instance, a number of excellent Japanese, French, German, Caribbean, and Asian restaurants as well as cultural centres and events representative of most of the world's people.

One of Toronto's 'Little Italies,' along St Clair Avenue.

MIRVISH VILLAGE

Mirvish Village is a small shopping area located on Markham Street, a block west of the intersection of Bathurst and Bloor streets. Restaurants, a very good art book store, and a number of other stores offer a distinctive and pleasant shopping experience. At the corner of Markham and Bloor stands a completely different shopping opportunity: Honest Ed's. This great, garish emporium is noted for its knockdown prices, tangle of floors and departments, and the fine art of shopping as a contact sport. Mirvish Village connects eastward to the heart of the city along Bloor Street. This section of Bloor is not as upscale as the more centrally-located part, but is an interesting area with its restaurants, book stores, and shops which cater to the local neighbourhood and the university crowd.

Surrounding Mirvish Village is one of the city's downtown residential neighbourhoods. Here, you can see typical Toronto Victorian and Edwardian domestic architecture. One of the city's best qualities is the fact that its downtown residential neighbourhoods have survived as healthy, well-populated, high quality communities in contrast to the more typical decline that sadly has characterized much of the rest of urban North America.

Upper: interesting shops and restaurants on Markham Street at Bloor.
Bottom: Honest Ed's - the great bargain basement landmark at the corner of Bloor and Bathurst.

The 1837 Regency cottage, Colborne Lodge, at the south end of High Park, open to the public as a historic house museum.

HIGH PARK AND COLBORNE LODGE

In 1873, John George Howard deeded his estate to the City of Toronto for a public park. That land, enlarged with other acquisitions, has led to the creation of one of Toronto's largest and most popular parks. High Park, located in the west end of the city, surrounded by an Edwardian residential neighbourhood, presents a variety of landscapes and recreational opportunities to the public.

The park's relatively undeveloped history, and its strategic location overlapping three distinct North American ecological zones, has created a unique opportunity for the naturalist to explore the indigenous Toronto environment: eastern deciduous forests from the south, prairie/savannah from the west, and boreal/mixed forest from the north. If you keep your eyes open to the subtle differences in the vegetation, the colours, and the 'feel' of the park, you should be able to spot the different zones as you pass through them. In addition to its natural attractions, High Park possesses features designed primarily to meet the recreational needs of

Torontonians. It has swimming pools, skating rinks, playing fields, picnic areas, a small children's zoo with bison, deer, and other animals, a duck pond, playgrounds, formal gardens, and an outdoor summer theatre.

High Park's most significant historic attraction is Colborne Lodge. Home of John George Howard and his wife Jemima, its period-room settings are furnished with the original Howard possessions, including the city's oldest flush toilet! Colborne Lodge is one of a number of restored historic houses in Toronto. Some of the others include: the 1832 Montgomery's Inn; the 1857 Mackenzie House; the c.1817 Grange; the 1820s Campbell House; and the 1866 Spadina.

High Park is located in the west end of the city. Its northern entrance is accessible from the Keele and High Park subway stations on the Bloor-Danforth line. The College 506 Streetcar enters the middle of the park, while the Queen 501 Streetcar passes close to the southern entrance.

This page and next: Casa Loma's eclectic architecture incorporates those elements of Norman, Gothic, and Romanesque design which appealed to the romantic tastes of its builder, Sir Henry Pellatt.

CASA LOMA

Casa Loma, 'the House on the Hill' is Toronto's great architectural folly, built between 1911-14 for one of the city's most romantic and flamboyant financiers, Sir Henry Pellatt. Today, Sir Henry's home is open to the public as a commercially-operated site where you can reminisce about the elegance of life for the rich in the Toronto of the 1910s and 1920s.

Born in 1859 in Kingston west of Toronto, Henry Pellatt was the son of a stockbroker. At age 17, young Henry went to Europe to drink in the antiques, the art, and the military traditions of the continent, all of which would dominate Henry's imagination and ultimately contribute to his downfall. However, tragedy lay in the future. As a young man Henry entered his father's business, joined Toronto's most prestigious militia regiment, became a renowned athlete, and married Mary Dodgson, a well-connected society woman. Land and stock speculation as well as investments in hydro-electric production, industrial endeavours in Brazil, and a host of other enterprises made Henry a rich man. Meanwhile, he rose in rank in his regiment, becoming commanding officer of the Queen's Own Rifles, and was given the title of *aide-de-camp* to the governor-general, Earl Grey. In 1905, King Edward VII knighted this ideal Edwardian gentleman, financier, and soldier. In 1910, at his own expense, Sir Henry transported 640 officers and men of the Queen's Own to England to participate in war games!

With his status and wealth, the time had come for Sir Henry to fulfil his youthful dreams of castles and actually build one on top of Davenport Hill overlooking the City of Toronto, complete with huge Tudoresque stables, a large beautiful garden, and even a deer park. Meanwhile, his peers in the conservative Canadian establishment thought Casa Loma a bit loud (and very un-Canadian) as well as more than a little pompous. Others were simply jealous. However, the thick-skinned Pellatt did not let opinion stop him, and he moved into his dream castle in 1914, a home which boasted 98 rooms, three bowling alleys, 30 bathrooms, an elevator, shooting gallery, wine cellar, pipe organ, and one of the first built-in vacuum systems.

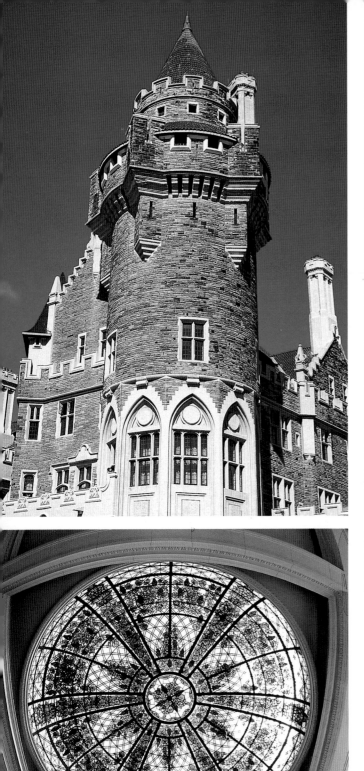

Upper: the Scottish and Norman towers, the latter with the recently-restored gardens in the foreground.
Lower: the Conservatory with its stained glass dome and marble floors and panels. Originally, the flower beds were heated with steam pipes to allow the Pellatts to grow exotic flowers.

Next page: upper: the serving room, used by the Pellatts for breakfast and other casual meals, now containing original Pellatt-family furniture; lower: the dining room for more formal events, such as Queen's Own Rifles officers' mess dinners.

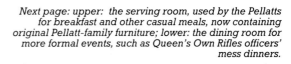

Upper: the Adams-style Round Room on the second floor.
Lower: Sir Henry's bedroom, with its mahogany and walnut walls.

Opposite: upper: Casa Loma's Great Hall with its 18-metre high ceiling; lower: the Oak Room with its French panels which took three years to carve.

Sadly, Sir Henry's glorious new life was not to last for long. World War I and the ensuing economic slump hurt Sir Henry's over-extended business interests. Fuel costs for the huge castle skyrocketed, as did maintenance, property taxes, and the salaries of his 40 servants. By 1924, the financially-strapped and publicly-embarrassed Sir Henry moved out and sold off most of his vast collection of antiques and furnishings. Lady Pellatt died that year; Sir Henry passed away in 1939.

Casa Loma survived as a hotel for a while before being taken over by the city in 1934 and then leased to the Kiwanis Club of West Toronto in 1937 to run as a tourist attraction. During World War II, the stables and carriage house were used secretly to assemble ASDIC, the new sonar submarine-detecting technology which proved so beneficial in the war against the U-boats in the Battle of the Atlantic.

Casa Loma is located at 1 Austin Terrace. If you're willing to hike up a very steep set of stairs, it is accessible from the Dupont Subway Station a few blocks to the south; otherwise approach it from the north, down Spadina Road from St Clair Avenue. As with all Toronto museums, phone ahead to confirm opening times.

This page: upper: the Great Hall; lower: the Carriage Room in Sir Henry's stables which can be reached through a 250-metre tunnel from the castle.

Opposite: Lady Mary Pellatt's suite which included a bedroom, sitting room, bathroom, and balcony, designed to make Sir Henry's semi-invalid wife as comfortable as possible.

Spadina, located immediately east of Casa Loma at 285 Spadina Road, is open as a historic house museum.

SPADINA

Next door to Casa Loma is a beautiful restored house that you should not miss, Spadina, the 1866 home of businessman and financier, James Austin. Owned by the City of Toronto and operated through the Toronto Historical Board, Spadina presents formal rooms where the Austins entertained their friends, such as the billiard room, dining room, and palm room; restored 'downstairs' features such as the kitchen, as well as the cosy upstairs spaces where the Austins retired to the privacy of their family lives. Furnished with an exceptional array of authentic family belongings, this gas-lit restoration presents the changing tastes of its owners in the Victorian and Edwardian eras.

Down in the basement, you can see the remains of earlier homes on the site through an interesting archaeological exhibit. Outside, the grounds boast one of Toronto's finest restored historic gardens which features more than 300 varieties of plants for your enjoyment.

Edwards Gardens, located at 777 Lawrence Avenue East at Leslie Street, not far from the Ontario Science Centre.

EDWARDS GARDENS

Public gardens are a long-standing tradition in Toronto. One of the more famous public gardens is Edwards Gardens. Hugging the Wilket Creek Ravine, Edwards Gardens present a huge variety of vegetation, presented in different formats, from formal gardens, to rockeries, to forested valley walls, to rose gardens. Some of the tree species include majestic black walnuts dating back to the first settlers' arrival on the site in the 1820s, mature deciduous and evergreen trees, birches, and hemlocks. As well, the Civic Garden Centre is located at Edwards Gardens. This facility is an internationally-recognized institution for the advancement of horticulture where you can take courses, seek gardening advice, consult its library, or browse through its gift and book shop.

Other public gardens include James Gardens on Edenbridge Drive, east of Royal York Road in the Toronto suburb of Etobicoke; and Rosetta McClain Gardens perched on Scarborough Bluffs off Kingston Road, west of Birchmount Road on the shore of Lake Ontario.

This page and opposite: high tech, hands-on, participatory educational fun are the hallmarks of the Ontario Science Centre.

ONTARIO SCIENCE CENTRE

Opened in 1969, the Ontario Science Centre has become one of Toronto's premier attractions. A whole generation of parents and children have grown up with the centre's ever-changing, hands-on exhibits and programmes. The Science Centre sits along the side of a steep, woodland hill over-looking the Don Valley. Begun in 1964, a fundamental idea behind the centre's creation was to break away from the traditional, artifact-centred, science museum in favour of what then was a revolutionary approach: exhibits with which you could interact and thus personally discover science for yourself. Operated by the Province of Ontario, the Science Centre has become famous for its ongoing programme of special exhibits in addition to its ever-changing core galleries and daily science demonstrations.

With an Omnimax Theatre and 650 exhibits devoted to such topics as the living earth, space, the body, communications, food, transportation, and other themes, a visit to the Science Centre is a full-day, family-oriented experience not to be missed.

The Ontario Science Centre is located in the east suburban region of the city. To get there by car, take the Don Valley Parkway to Don Mills Road North, then follow the signs to the centre at 770 Don Mills Road. By public transit, either take the Eglinton East Bus from the Eglinton Subway Station on the Yonge Line, or the Don Mills Bus from the Pape Subway Station on the Bloor-Danforth Line.

This page and next: some of the new friends you'll meet at the Metro Zoo.

METRO TORONTO ZOO

The Metro Toronto Zoo is one of the world's great zoos. Located on almost 300 hectares of land, the zoo has attracted millions of visitors since it opened in 1974. Its basic design is a 'zoogeographic' concentration of animals and plants in groupings which approximate the natural habitat of the animals. Different world zones presented in both pavilion and outdoor exhibits include Africa, Australasia, Eurasia, the Americas, Indo-Malaya, and Canada. All told, you can see 5000 animals, from giant elephants, lions, and bears, to tiny reptiles, birds, and bats.

The zoo's public amenities include restaurants, picnic areas, a monorail, and a gift shop (where you even can buy the zoo's own 'homemade' fertilizer, 'ZooPoo'). The zoo, open throughout the year, is located in northeast Scarborough, Toronto's easternmost suburb. Allow a full day to see the sites. By car, take Highway 401 to Meadowvale Road, then drive north, following the signs. There also is bus service from the Kennedy Subway Station on the Bloor-Danforth line, although it takes a while to get there from the subway.

The tinsmith's shop with a historic Masonic Lodge upstairs.

Opposite: historic workshops, stores, and craft demonstrations bring mid-Victorian Canada alive at Black Creek.

BLACK CREEK PIONEER VILLAGE

'Life in the Past Lane': that is the advertising motto of Black Creek Pioneer Village. And a good motto it is, because this is the place to come and spend a day living in the 1860s.

The settlement of Black Creek Pioneer Village goes back to 1816 when a Pennsylvanian-German family moved to the area and began the back-breaking work of carving out a home in the dense forest. Today, their first small, log house sits on the site, as does their second and larger, clapboard covered home, and some of their other buildings, built between 1816 and 1832. In recent decades, the Metropolitan Toronto and Region Conservation Authority preserved these structures and assembled about 40 other historic buildings near them to create an ethnographic village devoted to preserving the character of southern Ontario back in the 1860s. These buildings have been restored and furnished with a wonderful collection of artifacts, thus providing a fine opportunity to journey back in time.

The village, animated by costumed historical interpreters, possesses the typical range of buildings found in a 19th-century village: homes, churches, shops, mills, stores, inns, barns, and the outbuildings so common to the old rural landscape, as well as gardens, fields, and livestock. One of the more cerebral highlights is an early Mennonite meeting house where you can imagine the humble piety of this old Anabaptist denomination. A fascinating, but more dramatic building is Roblin's Mill, a large stone structure where you can see and hear the sounds of pre-industrial, water-powered manufacturing as its great stone wheels grind wheat into flour.

Black Creek Pioneer Village is located in the northwest corner of suburban Toronto, near the intersection of Jane Street and Steeles Avenue. Allow a full day to enjoy the village, and don't forget to visit the museum gallery and gift shop in the Visitor Centre too.

Canada's Wonderland boasts North America's greatest variety of roller coasters - nine in all; and that is only the beginning. There are dozens of other thrill rides, water amusements, and tamer rides for children, all located within a clean and attractive theme park environment.

CANADA'S WONDERLAND

Paramount Canada's Wonderland is a 148-hectare theme park located a bit north of Metropolitan Toronto off Highway 400. It is an island of dreams and fantasies, isolated from the real world, where you meet Fred Flintstone, Star Trek characters, enjoy theme villages, and thrill on its rides. Opened in 1981, the site is dominated by Wonder Mountain, an artificial hill with its popular Thunder Run water ride. There also are six theatres on the site where daily family-oriented performances take place and where, at the Kingswood Music Theatre, you can enjoy internationally-famous performers such as Fleetwood Mac, BB King, and the Beach Boys.

If you're looking for cultural attractions while north of Toronto, you will enjoy the superb collection of Group of Seven paintings at the McMichael

Canadiana Collection in Kleinburg, not far from Wonderland. About an hour and a half to the north and west is Ste-Marie-Among-the-Hurons in Midland, a recreated 17th-century French mission settlement with a very good museum which explores the age of European expansion and the indigenous culture of southern Ontario. About a kilometre from Ste-Marie is the Wye Marsh for the nature lover.

This page: Lester B. Pearson International Airport in Mississauga, just northwest of Toronto.
Opposite: upper: flying into the city; lower: Toronto City Centre Airport on the islands.

THE AIRPORTS

Toronto is served by two airports, the large Lester B. Pearson International Airport and the small Toronto City Centre Airport. Pearson Airport, originally founded as Malton Airport in 1937, is Canada's busiest, with 58 airlines servicing over 300 destinations in 60 countries around the world. Every year, 21,000,000 travellers use Pearson's three terminals.

If you have the choice, you might prefer to use the Toronto City Centre Airport. It is located at the west end of the Toronto Islands, and is accessible by ferry from the foot of Bathurst Street, just west of the central downtown, or via airline shuttle buses. Used by small commuter planes, the island airport can be much more convenient than Pearson for travelling to and from Ottawa, Montreal, and other centres. Opened in 1939 as Port George VI Airport, this facility served as a training centre for the Royal Norwegian Air Force in exile during World War II.

NIAGARA FALLS

Niagara Falls: one of the wonders of the world. Niagara Falls: an ever-changing natural phenomenon that has drawn people to admire their immense power for centuries. Niagara Falls: really three falls: the magnificent Canadian Horseshoe Falls, the impressive American Falls, and, a few metres away, the little Luna, or Bridal Veil falls. Niagara Falls: one of the most accessible of nature's great attractions, located less than a two-hour drive from Toronto along the Queen Elizabeth Way.

Fifteen thousand years ago, a layer of ice three kilometres thick lay on top of Ontario and New York. As the great ice sheet disappeared northwards, the Niagara River began to take shape. Now 12,000 years old, this 58-kilometre strait serves as the border between Canada and the United States between lakes Erie and Ontario. Every minute, 336,000 cubic metres of water enter the Niagara River from Lake Erie, representing the drainage accumulated from four of the Great Lakes which hold one-fifth of the world's supply of fresh

water, which they collect from a 684,000-square-kilometre watershed and send down the river to Lake Ontario and on to the Atlantic Ocean via the St Lawrence River. Today, half of the water is diverted to produce hydro-electric power while the other half crashes over the crest of the falls to thrill 12,000,000 visitors from around the globe every year.

In simplified form, the cliff this fabulous quantity of water crashes over consists of a hard top layer of dolomite limestone with softer layers of sandstone and shale underneath - the result of hundreds of millions of years of geological development. As the water falls over the edge, it eats away at the underlying soft rock, thus undermining the top layer until it collapses. This has been going on for the last 12,000 years. The result is that the falls have moved 11 kilometres upstream from their original position to the north. Five hundred years ago, there was only one waterfall which ran the entire width of the Niagara River, located about the site of today's American Falls. At that time, they ran into an immovable object, Goat Island. This caused the falls to split into two channels. Further erosion continued to shape them and give them their present-day shape. Until the 1950s, erosion took place at the rate of a metre a year; but recent human intervention has slowed the pace to about one metre every 30 years.

There are taller falls in the world, but only one is wider, Victoria Falls in Africa. Those at Niagara are about 20

Looking across the border from Canada towards the United States: in the foreground is the Table Rock House Plaza in Niagara Falls, Ontario, beside which are the Horseshoe Falls on the Canadian side of the Niagara River. In the background is Goat Island and the American and Bridal Veil falls in Niagara Falls, New York.

times as wide as they are tall, and the Niagara River under the falls is about as deep as the falls are high above the waterline. For example, the Horseshoe Falls are 52 metres above the waterline, 55 metres below.

Native peoples knew the falls for thousands of years and passed their knowledge on to the first European explorers in the early 17th century. The first eye-witness description of the falls appeared in print in 1683 when Louis Hennepin, a Recollet priest who accompanied La Salle on his journey in search of the Mississippi, published his memoirs. Viewing the cascading water, surrounded by the isolated glory of the primaeval forest, Hennepin marvelled how 'one is seized with Horror, and the Head turns round, so that one cannot look long or steadfastly upon it.' Later, in the 1750s, Swedish traveller Peter Kalm shared Hennepin's awe when he wrote, 'you cannot see it without being quite terrified.'

Few travellers came to the falls until the 1800s when the countryside around them began to fill up with settlers and transportation improved, first with the Erie Canal in the 1820s and then with the coming of railways in the middle decades of the century. By 1845, 100,000 tourists annually visited the falls and newly weds began to see them as an ideal honeymoon spot: they were less than a day's journey from some of the most populous regions in North America, they had a wide variety of hotels to meet every pocketbook, and, as most people hoped to see the falls at some time in their lives anyway, a honeymoon provided an ideal excuse to make the trip.

At the same time, entrepreneurs seized the opportunity to profit from the growing tourist trade. In 1818, William Forsyth on the Canadian side opened a special staircase so people could descend to the cataract below the falls to enjoy the terror and excitement of coming face to face with nature at its most powerful. In 1822 Forsyth opened a hotel beside the falls which competed with other businesses for tourists. As time went on, particularly by the 1860s and 1870s, the tourist industry at Niagara became something of a scandal. Prices were outrageous, service was terrible, and fraud was rampant. Rough characters offered 'free' admission to their seedy little attractions, but then threatened physical violence to extort large sums of money before they let unsuspecting tourists escape back into the sunlight. Similar problems ran rampant on the American side as well, while the additional menace of industrial development threatened to destroy the remaining beauty of the falls on the U.S. side in a frantic quest for cheap waterpower.

These problems forced governments on both sides of the border to expropriate the lands closest to the falls, turn them into parks, and operate them for the public benefit. In 1885, New York opened the first state park in American history while Ontario opened Canada's first provincial park in 1887. By about 1900, both jurisdictions had completed much of their work so the public could enjoy the glory of the falls in a verdant, peaceful, and controlled atmosphere, free from the hazards of old.

This page and opposite: in and about the falls.

Opposite: Victoria Park Restaurant, one of the Niagara Parks Commission's facilities where you can see the sights, dine, or shop (with the Skylon Tower in the background). This page: the Canadian Horseshoe Falls.

Next two pages: Horseshoe Falls from the air, with the International Control Dam behind them designed to reduce the erosion of the falls. Behind the dam are two early 20th-century hydro-electric generating stations.

CANADIAN FALLS

The Canadian side of the Niagara River has the most developed tourism facilities and the best views of the falls. At the centre of the tourism experience is Queen Victoria Park beside the falls, operated by the Government of Ontario through the Niagara Parks Commission.

Queen Victoria Park is where you go to see the falls in their full glory. The heart of the park is the Horseshoe Falls beside the Table Rock House Plaza. At the plaza, you can purchase souvenirs or snacks, get travel information, have dinner in a restaurant overlooking the falls, or go down below and behind the falls from the Journey Behind the Falls caves.

A little downriver, or north, of the falls, is the dock for the *Maid of the Mist* boat ride near the intersection of the Niagara Parkway and Clifton Hill. Farther north (a little more than four kilometres from the falls), beyond the Whirlpool Bridge, is the Great Niagara Gorge. At the gorge, you can descend an elevator to a river-level boardwalk and explore one of the world's wildest stretches of white water. Or, if you prefer the view from above, you can take a Spanish aerial cable car which passes over the spectacular Niagara whirlpool.

If you travel farther north along the Niagara Parkway (which runs parallel to the river), you can visit a number of other attractions run by the Parks Commission, including the Niagara Botanical Gardens with its butterfly conservatory (nine kilometres north of the falls), a floral clock (12 kilometres), and the preserved Queenston Heights Battlefield (13 kilometres) where British, Canadian, and Iroquois forces inflicted defeat on an invading American army in 1812 and where you can see the impressive 1853 monument to the hero of the battle, Sir Isaac Brock. Upriver, 500 metres south of the Horseshoe Falls, is the Niagara Parks Greenhouse and Fragrance Garden for those with horticultural interests.

Getting around to the Niagara Parks Commission's facilities is easy as the commission operates a very efficient and pleasant 'People Mover' shuttle bus between its attractions and the main parking lots. The falls, the restaurants, souvenir shops, *Maid of the Mist*, Journey Behind the Falls, Queenston Heights, and the greenhouse are open all year round. The shuttle bus and other attractions start operations in late April. The bus stops operating in early October, the gorge boardwalk closes in late October, the aerial car in late November.

This page and next: the Maids of the Mist *boats.*

THE *MAID OF THE MIST*

With the roar of the falls in their ears and the water spray in their faces, people have enjoyed donning protective rain gear and sailing aboard one of the *Maids of the Mist* into the heart of the Canadian Horseshoe Falls since 1846.

One of the sadder jobs of the *Maid of the Mist* boats is picking up the remains of suicides and other people who meet their doom in falling over the falls. However, in 1960, one of the boats had the happy task of rescuing a seven-year-old boy who fell into the Niagara River above the falls, wearing only a life jacket and bathing suit, and who was swept over the falls, but, miraculously, lived - the only unprotected person ever to have done so!

You can board one of the boats for the half-hour trip from a landing spot a bit north of the falls at 5920 River Road on the Canadian side of the Niagara River (near the Niagara Parkway and Clifton Hill, south of the Rainbow Bridge); or, on the American side, near the Observation Tower on Prospect Point. It's a very wet but exciting experience that you should not miss.

Opposite: upper: viewing the Horseshoe Falls on the Canadian side of the river from the Journey Behind the Falls outdoor observatory; all other pictures this page and opposite: down beside the American Falls at the Cave of the Winds Hurricane Deck.

CAVE OF THE WINDS
HURRICANE DECK
AND JOURNEY
BEHIND THE FALLS

No visit to Niagara Falls is complete without a trip down below and *behind* the falls where you can feel the full power of the vast quantities of water that pour over the falls every second!

On the Canadian side of the river, enter the Journey Behind the Falls (formerly the Table Rock Scenic Tunnels) from inside the Table Rock House complex beside the Horseshoe Falls. Once inside, you descend 38 metres in an elevator, put on your biodegradable souvenir raincoat, and walk through tunnels which have been carved out of the rock behind the falls so that you actually stand under and behind the falls. Magnificent! Then, wander outside onto the viewing platform for the soaking wet, but exhilarating experience of seeing the falls from below the great cliff.

Across the border on the American side, is the Cave of the Winds Hurricane Deck, accessible from Goat Island. There you can take a spectacular tour along special walkways to see the glory of the base of the American falls (although collapsing rocks prevent you from going behind the falls as people once were able to do). As in Canada, waterproof clothing is supplied for this wonderfully wet experience.

This page: the American Falls.
Opposite: the Canadian Horseshoe Falls.

Next pages: enjoy Niagara's night time illuminated glory all year round, a tradition that goes back to 1925.
Following two pages: a wide-angled view of the Canadian and American falls.

NIAGARA-ON-THE-LAKE

A trip to the Niagara River provides an excellent opportunity to sample the many interesting attractions in the Niagara region in addition to the falls. Perhaps the greatest gem is the 18th-century town of Niagara-on-the-Lake, located north of the falls on the Niagara Parkway at the mouth of the Niagara River. To get there, drive north from the falls for about 30 minutes until you reach this community, founded by United Empire Loyalist refugees from the American Revolution of 1775-83.

Niagara-on-the-Lake retains most of its historic charm and provides visitors with a number of cultural and historical opportunities. Its most famous annual event is the summer Shaw Festival, dedicated to the theatrical works of George Bernard Shaw and other dramatists. Historically, you might want to visit such sites as Fort George, Fort Mississauga, the Niagara Apothecary, or historic St Mark's Anglican and St Andrew's Presbyterian churches with their fascinating cemeteries. Alternatively, you just might want to wander around the historic streets or enjoy a fine meal in one of the town's restored inns, such as the Oban or the Prince of Wales, or you might choose to use Niagara-on-the-Lake as a base to tour the region's wineries.

AMERICAN FALLS

Although the attractions of the U.S. side are a bit more modest than those on the Canadian side of the Niagara River, there is much to see in Niagara Falls, New York, and a trip across the Rainbow Bridge to explore the falls from an American perspective is worth the effort.

Central to the American experience is Niagara Reservation State Park, a clean and wooded sanctuary in which you enjoy the falls in a more peaceful atmosphere than you can on the Canadian side. To get your bearings and a historical backgrounder to the site, visit the New York State Park Visitors' Center in the park, and don't miss its thrilling theatre presentation, 'Niagara Wonders.' For a bird's-eye-view of the Falls, climb to the top of the New York State Observation Tower for a dramatic perspective of all three falls: the American, Bridal Veil, and Canadian Horseshoe falls; or descend to its base to catch the *Maid of the Mist* boat tour. Afterwards, wander over or take the Park Viewmobile to Goat Island for a fabulous view of the Horseshoe Falls or an exploration of the falls from down below on the Cave of the Winds Deck . Alternatively, head north to the Schoellkopf Geological Museum for a study of the 450,000,000-year-old history of the region, located a short drive or a healthy walk north of the visitor centre.

116

Clockwise, opposite and this page: American Falls with the much narrower Bridal Veil (or Luna) Falls beside them; the 1941 Rainbow Bridge which replaced one destroyed by ice in 1938; the American Falls from Goat Island; looking towards Canada.

The Falls 'stopped' on two occasions in recorded history. The first time occurred for a short while in 1848 when freak winds and an ice jam upstream at Buffalo cut the flow of water, the second happened in 1969 when the United States Army dammed the channel leading to the American Falls and shut them off for a few months. In 1848, all sorts of people flocked onto the suddenly dry river bed to marvel at the unique opportunity to explore the falls. Others, fearful that the world was about to end, gathered in churches, only to have their anxieties relieved when the ice dam broke. The second time, the American government wanted to see if it could remove the rocks at the base of the American Falls to improve the appearance of the falls. In 1931 a huge chunk of the crest of the American Falls collapsed, destroying the straight fall that had existed before and piled up masses of rock at its base. During the 1969 exploration, the engineers concluded that the great 214,000-cubic-metre pile of rock was both a natural phenomenon in the evolution of the falls and played a critical role in keeping the rest of the falls up. Thus, they decided not to remove the rock before 'turning' the falls back on again.

This page and next: the American Falls.

OTHER ATTRACTIONS ON THE AMERICAN SIDE

As in Canada, the American side of the river has its attractions additional to the falls, whether it be a native cultural centre in Niagara Falls, outlet malls where designer clothes are sold at bargain-basement prices, the City of Buffalo to the south with its museums and attractions, or the historical, boating, and recreational facilities that dot the New York side of the Niagara Peninsula.

Three attractions closely related to the Niagara River lie north of Niagara Falls, New York along the river's edge. In Lewiston, you can visit the Niagara Power Project Visitors' Center and learn how Niagara's waterpower has been harnessed to generate hydroelectric power since the 1890s. Also in Lewiston is ArtPark, an 80-hectare site dedicated to the performing and visual arts where concerts, jazz, dance, and other presentations take place every summer. At the mouth of the Niagara River, outside the historic village of Youngstown, stands Old Fort Niagara, one of the best forts in the Great Lakes region, with a history going back to the late 17th century. Today, buildings as old as the 1720s stand behind its defensive walls which guarded French, British, and American garrisons throughout its long and violent history.

MINOLTA, KODAK, AND SKYLON TOWERS

In Queen Victoria Park, you can stand beside the crest of Niagara Falls, you can go below and behind the falls from the tunnels and platforms of Journey Behind the Falls, and you can sail almost into the falls aboard the *Maid of the Mist.* If you're still not content, then you can travel up the hill behind the park and ascend one of the towers overlooking the falls!

The Skylon Tower (near Murray Street and Oakes Drive) boasts both indoor and outdoor observation decks 236 metres above the falls with a 125 kilometre view, as well as a buffet dining room, and a revolving restaurant at the top. At the base, the Skylon offers shops and the largest amusement arcade in Niagara Falls. The Minolta Tower (near Portage Road South and Oakes Drive, and accessible from Queen Victoria Park on an inclined railway) is a newly-renovated facility which, like the Skylon, offers observation decks, dining, and various forms of family entertainment, as does the Kodak Tower which forms part of Maple Leaf Village near Clifton Hill and Falls Avenue. If you still are not satisfied with the view, then you should go for a Helicopter Ride over the falls at 3731 Victoria Avenue, off the Niagara Parkway, north of falls.

Opposite: upper: Skylon Tower behind the Victoria Restaurant; lower: enjoying the view from on high.
This page: upper: Kodak Tower at Maple Leaf Village;
lower: Minolta Tower.

CLIFTON HILL

Back in the 1880s, when the government of Ontario created Queen Victoria Park along the edge of the Niagara River, the idea was to rid Niagara Falls of the hucksters who had been giving the province's foremost attraction a bad name. Although more respectable than they were in the 1880s, the hucksters never went away. Instead, they retreated up Clifton Hill where they now invite you to partake of the peculiar charms of their own attractions.

Typical of the commercial sites of Clifton Hill is Louis Tussaud's Waxworks where, as you might expect, you can see models of Henry VIII and other members of the British Royal Family, world leaders, movie stars, Mother Theresa, and the inevitable Mediaeval Torture Chamber. High culture it ain't; but it can be fun. Other 'museums' include the Ripley Believe it or Not! Museum and the Guinness World of Records Museum. The granddaddy of them all is the Niagara Falls Museum (located a short distance from Clifton Hill). It dates back to 1827 and offers a melange of mummies, freaks of nature, and the Niagara Daredevils Hall of Fame, dedicated to people who sought renown by sailing over the falls inside barrels and other, equally insane contraptions.

This page and next: the honky-tonk dazzle of Clifton Hill.

124

Black Creek
Pioneer Village

Canada's
Wonderland

St. Clair Ave. West

St.Clair Ave. West

St. Clair

Dundas St. West

St. John's Rd.

Davenport Rd.

Dupont

Annette

Keele St.

Keele St.

Dundas St. West

Caledonia Pk. Rd.

Lansdowne Ave.

Via Italia

Dufferin St.

Dovercourt Rd.

Ossington Ave.

Daven

Bloor St. West

Bloor St. West

High Park

Howard Park Ave.

Parkside Dr.

Roncesvalles Ave.

Dundas St. West

Lansdowne Ave.

College St.

Dufferin St.

Dovercourt Rd.

Ossington Ave.

Grenadier Pond

Colborne
Lodge

The Queensway

Gardiner Expwy.

Lake Shore Blvd. West

King St.

Queen St. West

Jameson Ave.

Dufferin St.

West

Dufferin St.

Dovercourt Rd.

Ossington Ave.

Queen St. West

Sudbury St.

King

LAKE

Gardiner Expwy.

Lake Shore Blvd. West

Exhibition
Place

Strachan

Ontario
Place

ONTARIO

Woodbridge

Thornhill

North
York

Malton

Scarborough

York

Etobicoke

City of
Toronto

East York

LAKE ONTARIO

1   0,5   0   1 km

0,5   0,25   0   0,5   1 Mile

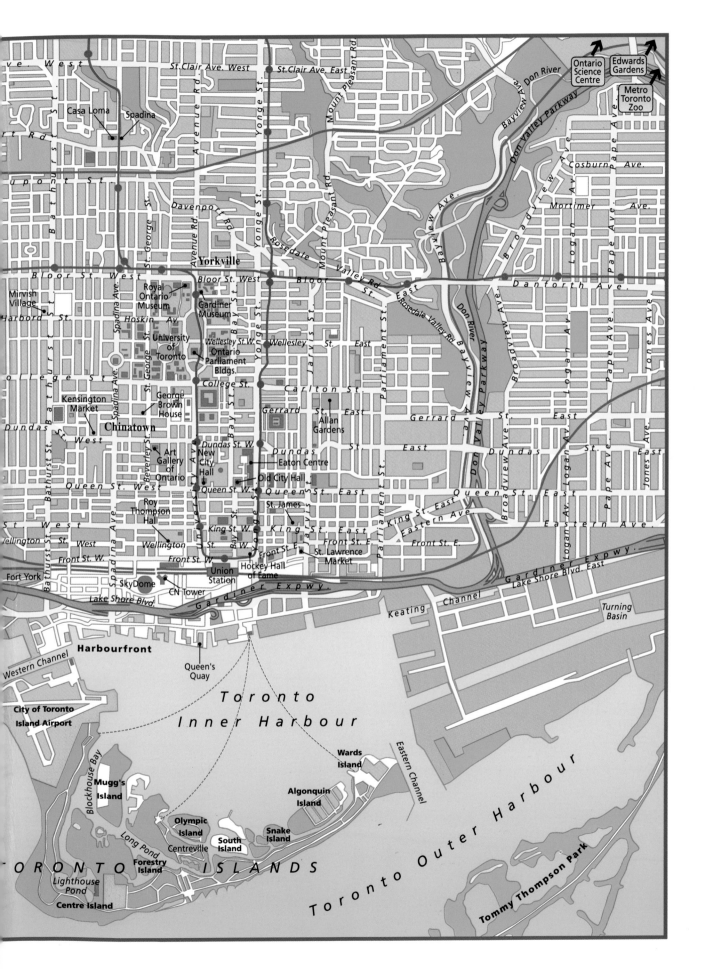

St. Clair Ave. West   St. Clair Ave. East

ve. West

Casa Loma
Spadina

Ontario
Science
Centre

Edwards
Gardens

Metro
Toronto
Zoo

Cosburn   Ave.

Mortimer   Ave.

Davenport Rd.

Yorkville

Bloor St. West   Bloor St. West   Bloor   St.   East   Danforth   Ave.

Mirvish
Village

Royal
Ontario
Museum

Gardiner
Museum

Hoskin   Av.

University
of
Toronto

Wellesley St. W.   Wellesley   St.   East

Ontario
Parliament
Bldgs.

College St.   Carlton   St.

Kensington
Market

George
Brown
House

Gerrard   St.   East   Gerrard   St.   East

Chinatown

Allan
Gardens

Dundas   West

Dundas St. W.   Dundas   East   Dundas

Art
Gallery
of
Ontario

New City
Hall

Eaton Centre

Old City Hall

Queen St. West   Queen St. W.   Queen   St. East   Queen St. East

Roy
Thompson
Hall

St. James

King St. East

Eastern Ave.

St West   Wellington   St.   West   King St. W.   King   St. East   Eastern   Ave.

Wellington

Front St. W.   Front St. E.   Front St. E.   Front St. E.

Fort York

SkyDome   Union
Station

Hockey Hall
of Fame

St. Lawrence
Market

Lake Shore Blvd.   CN Tower   Gardiner   Expwy.

Keating   Channel

Gardiner   Expwy.

Lake Shore Blvd. East

Turning
Basin

Western Channel

Harbourfront

Queen's
Quay

Toronto
Inner Harbour

City of Toronto
Island Airport

Wards
Island

Eastern Channel

Mugg's
Island

Algonquin
Island

Toronto Outer Harbour

Olympic
Island

Snake
Island

Centreville

South
Island

ORONTO   ISLANDS

Forestry
Island

Tommy Thompson Park

Lighthouse
Pond

Centre Island

INDEX

TORONTO
INTRODUCTION . . . . .page 3

Airports . . . ." 96
Allan Gardens Conservatory . . . ." 64
Art Gallery of Ontario . . . ." 49
Bata Shoe Museum . . . ." 73
Black Creek Pioneer Village . . . ." 92
Bloor Street West . . . ." 74
Canada's Wonderland . . . ." 94
Casa Loma . . . ." 78
Centreville . . . ." 29
Chinatown . . . ." 47
CN Tower . . . ." 17
Colborne Lodge . . . ." 77
Eaton Centre . . . ." 56
Edwards Gardens . . . ." 87
Exhibition Place . . . ." 36
Ferries . . . ." 27
Financial District . . . ." 60
George Brown House . . . ." 48
George R. Gardiner Museum
  of Ceramic Art . . . ." 73
Harbourfront . . . ." 23
High Park . . . ." 77
Historic Fort York . . . ." 40
Hockey Hall of Fame . . . ." 60
Kensington Market . . . ." 47
Little Italy . . . ." 75
Metro Toronto Zoo . . . ." 90
Mirvish Village . . . ." 76
New City Hall . . . ." 52
Old City Hall . . . ." 54
Ontario Parliament Buildings . . . ." 65
Ontario Place . . . ." 35
Ontario Science Centre . . . ." 88

Queen Street West . . . . .page 48
Queen's Quay . . . ." 23
Railway Lands . . . ." 15
Roy Thompson Hall . . . ." 50
Royal Ontario Museum . . . ." 68
St James Cathedral . . . ." 62
St Lawrence Market . . . ." 63
SkyDome . . . ." 9
Spadina . . . ." 86
Theatres . . . ." 59
Toronto Harbour . . . ." 33
Toronto Islands . . . ." 25
Union Station . . . ." 60
University of Toronto . . . ." 66
Yonge Street . . . ." 56
Yorkville . . . ." 74

Map . . . ." 126

NIAGARA FALLS
INTRODUCTION . . . ." 98

American Falls . . . ." 116
Canadian Falls . . . ." 103
Cave of the Winds Hurricane Deck . . . ." 109
Clifton Hill . . . ." 124
Journey Behind the Falls . . . ." 109
Kodak Tower . . . ." 123
Maid of the Mist . . . ." 106
Minolta Tower . . . ." 123
Niagara-on-the-Lake . . . ." 111
Other Attractions on the American side . . . . . ." 120
Skylon Tower . . . ." 123